KATE RIGGS

grow with me

TOMATO

CREATIVE EDUCATION

Published by Creative Education
P.O. Box 227, Mankato, Minnesota 56002
Creative Education is an imprint of
The Creative Company
www.thecreativecompany.us

Design and production by Ellen Huber
Art direction by Rita Marshall
Printed in the United States of America

Photographs by Alamy (amana images inc., Daniel
Dempster Photography, Pegaz, Star Pix), Corbis (Jerome
Wexler/Visuals Unlimited), Dreamstime (Amineimo,
Dusan Kostic, Lianem, Sgoodwin4813, Wellford
Tiller), Getty Images (Taylor S. Kennedy), iStockphoto
(Liudmila Chernova, Kitty Ellis, emmgunn, Tobias
Helbig, Jim Jurica, Viktor Kitaykin, Le Do, MorePixels,
Don Nichols, rphotos), Science Photo Library (ZEISS),
Shutterstock (Smit), Veer (Calek, dobdesign, jabiru,
Mirage3, Alexey Stiop, tuja66)

Library of Congress Cataloging-in-Publication Data
Riggs, Kate.
Tomato / Kate Riggs.
p. cm. — (Grow with me)
Includes bibliographical references and index.
Summary: An exploration of the life cycle and life span
of tomatoes, using up-close photographs and step-by-
step text to follow a tomato's growth process from seed
to seedling to mature plant.

ISBN 978-1-60818-219-0
1. Tomatoes—Life cycles—Juvenile literature.
2. Tomatoes—Seeds—Juvenile literature. I. Title.
SB349.R54 2012
641.3'5642—dc23   2011040502

CPSIA: 021413 PO1656
9 8 7 6 5 4 3 2

TABLE OF CONTENTS

Tomatoes are annual plants. Annuals are plants that live for a year or less. They grow from seeds. Tomatoes grow best in **fertile** soil that gets plenty of water. They need a lot of sunlight, too.

Tomatoes are **native** to South America. There they are perennial plants. This means that they can live and grow year round. Tomato plants have vines that can be 3 to 10 feet (0.9–3 m) long.

4

Tomatoes are fruits,
but sometimes
people think of
them as vegetables.

5

6 *All tomatoes are green at first. Then some change color.*

The tomato is a flowering plant that produces fruits. The seeds are found in the fruit. Tomato fruit is usually red and round. But some tomatoes are orange, yellow, or even green. Tomatoes can also be shaped like ovals and pears.

The seed is the beginning of a tomato. A seed must be planted to grow. Many people first plant tomato seeds in pots. They keep the pots indoors where it is warm. The seed starts to **germinate** (*JER-mih-nate*) about 5 to 10 days after it is planted.

7

The root is part of the embryo and grows outside the seed coat.

8 A seed is dry. Inside the seed is an **embryo** (*EM-bree-oh*). The embryo is wrapped in a hard shell called a seed coat. Water softens the seed coat. Then the embryo gets bigger and breaks through the seed coat.

The seed's root grows down into the soil. Its seed coat comes off, and the first leaves appear. This plant is called a seedling.

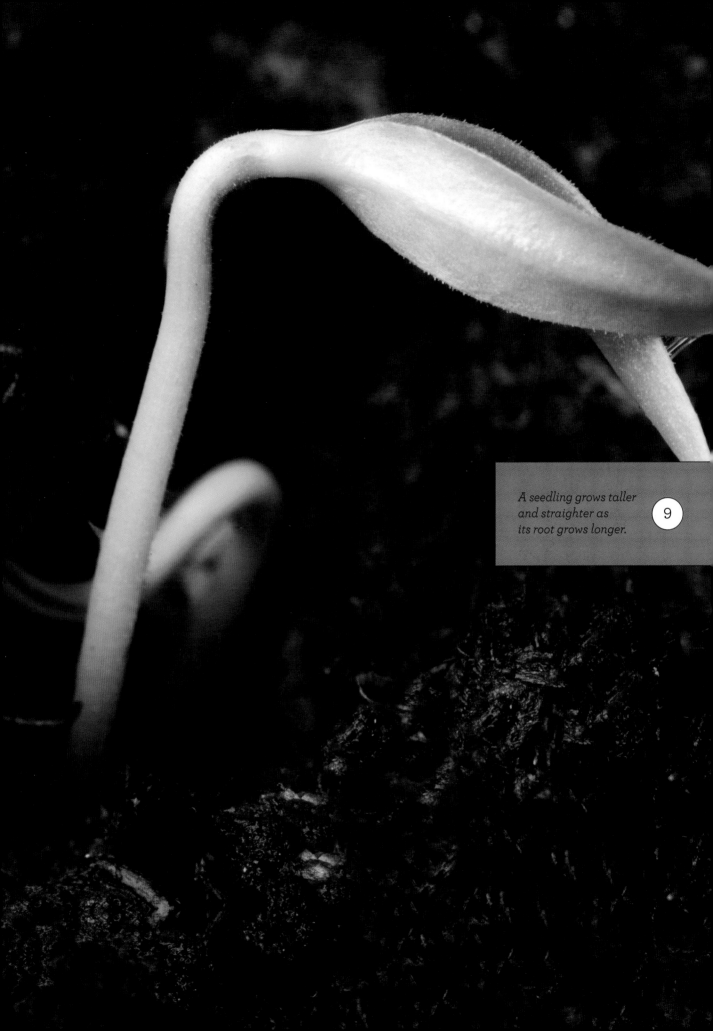

A seedling grows taller and straighter as its root grows longer.

9

Seedlings may be planted in mesh bags to give roots room to grow.

A seedling has three parts. The root is the first part. Then the shoot grows up out of the soil. The leaves branch off from the shoot. Tomato seedlings have leaves in pairs. Tomato plants belong to a group of flowering plants called dicots.

Light gives the seedling energy. Tomato seedlings need strong light for 16 to 18 hours a day. Air helps the seedling produce more energy to keep growing. A seedling uses light, air, and water to make food for itself.

11

leaf

stem

roots

12 *Tomatoes can be grown anywhere in the world that has the right conditions.*

A few days after it sprouts, a tomato seedling may still have the seed coat hanging on. The coat falls away as the leaves open fully. Seedlings grow best at a temperature of about 65 °F (18 °C).

After about 10 days, there are many leaves on the seedling. It is light green, and the leaves have tiny hairs on them. The plant grows straight up into the air.

13

A tomato cage is made out of strong metal or wire.

14 In places where winter is cold, a seedling from a pot can be **transplanted** after the last **frost**. The plant will die if it gets too cold. It needs to be planted deep in the soil. The seedling's roots will need to grow long.

The seedling grows more leaves and gets taller. Some people put a tomato cage around the plant when it is about 12 inches (30.5 cm) tall. The cage will support the vines and keep the plant from spreading over the ground.

A plant that started in a pot can have a lot of roots bunched up together.

15

16 *The yellow petals of the tomato flower are called the corolla.*

About a month after it has been planted in the ground, a tomato plant starts to flower. Tomato flowers are small and yellow. They have **pollen** inside them. The flowers drop pollen during the day.

The wind picks up the pollen and **pollinates** other tomato flowers. People can help tomato plants pollinate by shaking them gently. Moving the plant a little bit once or twice a week helps release more pollen.

17

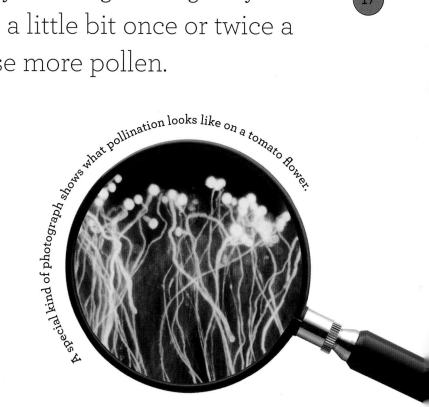

A special kind of photograph shows what pollination looks like on a tomato flower.

Once the tomatoes are pollinated, flowers can turn into fruit. Fruit starts to appear 45 to 90 days after transplanting. At first, the fruit is small and green.

It takes about four to six weeks for the fruit to **ripen**. One plant can produce about 15 tomatoes in a season. Plants with smaller fruits can hold many more than 15 tomatoes.

18

Tomatoes need to be watered to help the fruits grow bigger.

19

The ripest tomatoes on this plant are a dark red color.

20

Birds with talons, or sharp claws, can hold on to a round tomato.

21

People pick tomatoes when the color of the fruit starts to change. A red tomato starting to get pink is ripe enough to pick. A tomato's color will get darker as it ripens. Picked tomatoes should be stored in a cool place until they are ready to eat.

Tomatoes that stay on the vines too long get mushy. Animals such as squirrels, birds, and deer like to eat some tomatoes. The leaves on a tomato plant wither and die in the fall.

People grow tomatoes so they can eat them. Tomatoes can be sliced up for sandwiches. Small tomatoes can be eaten whole in salads. Other tomatoes can be made into sauces, pastes, and ketchup.

It is okay to eat the seeds in a tomato. But many tomato seeds are taken out of the fruit to grow more tomato plants. A jellylike **pulp** surrounds the seeds and protects them.

22

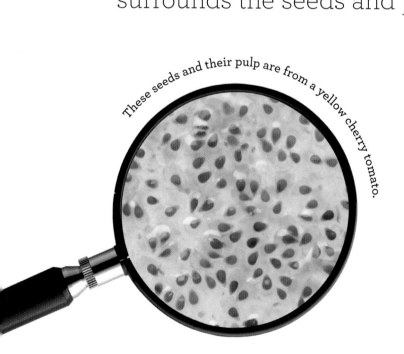

These seeds and their pulp are from a yellow cherry tomato.

Tomatoes do not need to be peeled or seeded before being eaten.

23

24

*There are about
10,000 different kinds
of tomato grown
in the world today.*

People in Mexico started growing tomatoes almost 1,400 years ago. They found out that they liked the taste of juicy tomatoes. Before that, tomatoes grew **wild** in South America.

In the 1500s, people in Europe (*YOO-rup*) first learned about tomatoes. Some people thought the fruits were **poisonous**. They grew tomatoes just to look at them.

25

Today, people plant tomatoes in fields, gardens, and **greenhouses**. They first plant seeds in pots. The seeds need a sunny place to grow and lots of water.

The seed begins to sprout. Soon it is a seedling. When the seedling gets too big for the pot, it is planted in the warm ground. Some tomato plants reach a certain height and stop growing. Others will keep producing vines and fruits for a longer time.

26

Seedlings that are grown indoors need to be watered regularly.

The largest tomato plant ever measured had vines that were 65 feet (20 m) long.

Tomatoes grow and ripen until the soil gets too dry or until the first frost. They usually do not last through the winter. The same tomato plant will not come back the following spring. A new seed will be planted. It will sprout leaves and make fruits of its own.

28

Tomatoes can be preserved, or kept for a long time, in jars.

A dead tomato plant turns brown and dries out.

29

A seed is planted in a pot in the spring.

The seed  begins to germinate in 5 to 10 days.

The seedling grows for several weeks.

The seedling is transplanted in the soil outdoors.

After 30 or more days, a tomato plant starts to flower.

The plant is pollinated by the wind.

Fruit appears 45 to 90 days after transplantation.

Fruit ripens for another 4 to 6 weeks.

Tomatoes are picked, and the plant dies in the fall.

embryo: *the part of a seed that grows into a plant*

fertile: *able to help things grow*

frost: *a time of colder weather when ice forms and plants stop growing*

germinate: *start to grow*

greenhouses: *buildings made of glass that are used to grow plants*

native: *from a certain place*

poisonous: *causing death or illness*

pollen: *a yellow powder made by flowers that is used to fertilize other flowers*

pollinates: *takes pollen from one flower to another to fertilize the plant, causing seeds to grow*

pulp: *the soft, wet inside part of a fruit*

ripen: *become ripe, or ready for picking and eating*

transplanted: *replanted in another place, such as from a pot to the ground*

wild: *living on its own; not grown by people*

WEB SITES

DLTK's Crafts for Kids: Tom the Tomato
http://www.dltk-kids.com/nutrition/mtomato.html
Print out and color a picture of a tomato named Tom.

The Tomato Zone
http://www.thetomatozone.co.uk/
Learn more about tomatoes and how they grow in greenhouses.

READ MORE

Landau, Elaine. *Tomatoes.*
New York: Children's Press, 1999.

Snyder, Inez. *Tomatoes.*
New York: Children's Press, 2004.